To the Land of
TEA AND TURRETS

A TEEN'S MEMOIR

ANNA MARIA TOMS

INDIA • SINGAPORE • MALAYSIA

ISBN 979-8-89277-977-7

A YOUNG TRAVELER SPEAKS

Paul Zacharia

Anna's travelogue, as all good travelogues do, carries the readers along with her and makes them feel they're part of her journey. Her observant eyes pick out unexpected details from the world she's exploring and at the same time keep watching light-heartedly the ways of her companions. She's an inquisitive traveler – as any good traveler should be – who tries to understand why a country and its people are the way they are. She's up-to-date on the history that's behind the things she's looking at it. Anna's style is personal, engaging and clear. She ably presents a transparent, entertaining and informed view of the place she's traveling in.

In this winningly narrated book we find her in Great Britain on a first visit along with her family and grandparents. Starting with the unexpected flight cancellation at the Bangalore airport and the ensuing confusion, she moves to a description of the flight next day via the busy Abu Dhabi hub to Manchester where her uncle, who's their host, lives. Anna quickly begins to take in life in Britain which is of course vastly different from ours in many ways. She calmy takes note of the British way of life which she is experiencing for the first time, and her outlook is sometimes critical and sometimes appreciative. She notes how the neighborhood church was small and, unlike in India, without any gaudy ornamentation – except a small cross- it was the Easter season. And the church was nearly empty. Anna writes: 'I always liked the idea of a simple church with an interior free from shiny distractions and this was often difficult to find in the place I came from.' They had landed in England in the middle of spring but even then she finds the cold hard to bear and regrets how the clothing she has to wear to protect her from the cold, takes away the freedom to enjoy an outing.

Her travels – along with her family of course – take her nearly across the whole length and breadth of Great Britain. From Manchester, a city she appreciates for its architecture, they proceed to Lake district, famous for its outstandingly beautiful landscape made all the more famous by its great son, poet William Wordsworth. They of course make the pilgrimage to Wordsworth's house and in Grasmere have a taste of the famed gingerbread. Looking at the sheep grazing in the meadows Anna is reminded of the sheep Dolly, world's first cloned mammal, who was born in nearby Scotland. She writes, 'Unlike the rest of the sheep that moved about, she was unlucky as she had to spend her entire life in a closed space under the supervision of many people. How difficult it must have been for her to stay away from such alluring green fields with plenty of fresh grass to feed on?'

And they then proceed to Scotland, the land of lochs, glens, mountains, rolling hills, woodlands and grassy plains. It was very, very cold yet they had a look, among other famous sights, at the Loch Ness and naturally Anna's mind wanders to the mythical Loch Ness Monster. In Edinburgh they have a wonderful time exploring the historical monuments. The only experience the party did not relish in Scotland was the claustrophobic hotel they had checked into. After visiting Glasgow, Anna and co have a look at the Roman Baths, the history of which Anna narrates in detail.

Later they move on to Stone Henge, the mysterious prehistoric circle of stone that stands like the centennial of a secret past – a conundrum not yet resolved. Their next stop is Portsmouth where they enjoy warm Malayali hospitality, making them forget all the turmoil of the journey. And Anna fondly recalls that this was where the master storyteller Charles Dickens was born. Then they are in London, the fabled city celebrated in history, literature and cinema, an extraordinary confluence of races, languages and cultures. They take in all the well-known sights of London such as the ancient Westminster Abbey and the modern London Eye; and the Tower of London and Madame Tussaud's. Anna is enthralled by the city. She writes, 'The London rush unfolded before my eyes, a scene never lacking in vibrancy. People filled the iconic red double-decker buses, taxis zipped by, and everything seemed to move swiftly around us.'

Another memorable visit she makes is to the hallowed pilgrimage place of the world of literature, Stratford-upon-Avon, the birth place of William Shakespeare. Anna remembers how 'the bare, shriveled branches' of the trees in the church yard creaked as they went to visit the Bard's grave. They also visit Wales and Liverpool and a few more places of interest. And finally it is time to return. Anna writes: 'My eyes teared up. I was happy that the trip turned better than how I anticipated and there was a part of me that knew I would miss that place.'

Anna's first travelogue is a delectable read. It is fascinating to see how a young traveler discovers a new and unfamiliar world and how she heartily enjoys the experience and also ruminates about it at the same time. The cheerful illustrations in color add to its attractiveness. Intelligent, thoughtful and observant, Anna's first travelogue, let's hope, will be the starting point of many more.

CHAPTER 1

Superstitions, often associated with objects or events that bring ill fortune or unexplainable coincidences, have mysterious origins. It's speculated that these beliefs might have stemmed from tales shared in remote villages a long time ago, where gatherings under banyan trees were common. Picture this scene: a remote location far from the sound of mooing cows, with a banyan tree's hanging roots swaying gently in the night breeze. People would gather here to discuss various matters, share stories, and sometimes even boast about their day's accomplishments. A kerosene lamp at the centre of their assembly would cast a soft glow, allowing them to read each other's expressions while narrating stories. Could it be that these storytelling sessions played a role in sparking superstitions? The answer remains uncertain, but I hope to shed some light on this as the story unfolds.

Now, you might be wondering why I'm delving into the topic of superstitions and their origins when I should be sharing my travel experiences. You will soon understand my reason as I reveal the answers to these questions, and you might find yourself questioning whether these beliefs are real or mere coincidences.

It was April 19, 2019, Good Friday, a day of great biblical significance as it commemorates the crucifixion of Jesus. However, the title "Good Friday" seems paradoxical, considering it's a day of mourning. From where I stood, I observed my maternal grandfather, Appachan, seated in an airport chair not far from the counter, engrossed in his reading material. A few minutes passed, and I turned to take another glance at him. This time, he looked back at me with a wrinkled, confused expression. Did he understand why we were being made to wait?

Appachan, in his late seventies, had fairly good eyesight even without his glasses, but he pulled out his pair to get a better picture of the scene. This was one of the many things he carried in his shirt's pocket. But the glasses were used sparingly.

He attributed his strong eyes to an Ayurvedic eye drop, claiming it contained rare herbs which promised numerous benefits, along with a healthy dose of luck. His essentials were minimal and could fit into his shirt's pocket, whether for everyday use or special occasions. These essentials included a button phone, black-rimmed glasses, sometimes a wristwatch (if it was not worn around his wrist), some cash, and a pen. Like most seventy-year-olds, even he did not require a comb. This, of course, to his benefit, was one thing less to worry about!

He got up from the recliner seat and walked up to us, holding a new magazine issue. He could smell serious trouble even though the voice of the counter staff barely reached him and surmised that the worst that could have happened to the trip had happened. The five of us now stood in a corner, watching the busy airport crowd. In ten minutes, it was our turn again. The lady in the pinstripe suit beckoned to us. A fun scarf with a complex knot showed from her shirt's collar, and her hair was neatly put up in a bun. She examined our passports but halted at a particular page, her eyes fixed on it. Something about it puzzled her. Was it just that the passports required scrutiny, or was there an issue with our tickets? We were left in the dark as she quickly jotted down a note and left the scene.

Tension mounted as we were left to our own devices, devoid of any explanation. It was evident that something was wrong, but the lady returned without saying a word and awaited someone. A middle-aged man, whom I deemed the "mystery man," eventually appeared beside her in an expensive suit. He was short with a round but firm gut, and it seemed like his belly movements synchronised with his speech's intonations. The further motion was restricted by the buttons of his blazer, which would have lost its ability to hold everything in place with the repetitive inhales and exhales that were forced outward. He had to provide an explanation for a serious matter, and because of this, I doubted if the buttons would survive much longer. "I am afraid you won't be able to fly today because your visa starts only tomorrow," he said in a booming voice, ruining the excitement.

With those few words, the tension in the air returned in full force, and panic set in. Confused glares and scowls from the people in the queue followed us as we retreated to the recliner seats. Alas! The broken glass had done its job.

I leaned forward, cupping my face in my hands. My mind drifted back to how it all began. It was the midst of March, and the scorching summer heat had already arrived. Instead of burying myself in a stack of books for my final revision, I found myself daydreaming. The windows were wide open, causing the fearfully hot breeze to gush in. The fan ran at its maximum, the curtains bellowed wildly, and the coconut trees moved their withered branches with the wind. My throat was parched and my clothes sweaty, but these handicaps didn't stop me from daydreaming like any child dearly waiting for the holidays would do. *"How nice it is to think of the holidays when you are nowhere close to it!"* I thought while treating myself to a few hot banana fritters that came straight from Amma's kitchen. *"Plenty of things had to be done in a short span of one month,"* I thought for the umpteenth time as I completed my snack. The tickets had to be booked, the itinerary had to be made, and before anything, I had to get over with my exams. No school, no homework, and no more boring business for almost an entire month. That is how everything turns out in the beginning, but reality strikes the very next day when you are sitting idle, gazing at the rusty fans of your house or unwillingly doing the chores that you have been keeping aside.

I contemplated the upcoming holidays, eagerly awaiting the break from school, homework, and routine chores. But summer had its own charms. Ripe mangoes hanging from the branches of mango trees, including one in our front yard, were a common sight. The tree provided shade, and when the time was right, it bore plump, mature mangoes. The tree's elevated position allowed it to showcase its offerings, attracting not only passers-by but also local schoolchildren. Some were skilled at aiming and returned with a good haul, while others were less fortunate. Those that fell were left to rot, providing no benefit to birds or children, a disappointing sight indeed.

As the mangoes began to take on a yellow tint, they would disappear. It would remain a mystery until they would make their appearance once again, this time pickled in glass bottles kept at children's stalls. Summer activities dating back to my parents' and grandparents' time weren't any less fun. It involved town exploration in groups, building playhouses from lightweight branches, and playing hide and seek. Ceiling fans were a luxury only a few could afford during those times. Beating the heat meant taking dips in ponds shaded from the sun or plunging into rivers. Those who didn't swim would sit on the large rocks by the water's edge, some of which had rocky puddles, though these were often avoided due to fears of mosquito breeding. The river's flowing water was fresh and safe, though strong currents could lead to accidents. I had a deep fascination for hearing stories of those times, with Appa and Amma providing vivid descriptions that painted a clear picture in my mind. However, things had changed over the years, and Appachan and I lamented that people no longer took pleasure in life's simple joys.

During the summer, my idle time away from travelling was filled with daydreams. With the holidays ahead and excitement building, the days seemed to drag, leaving me with one pressing question: *"When will the holidays finally arrive?"* But soon, my thoughts would shift to the less enjoyable aspect of travel: packing. In my memory, packing was never an enjoyable task; it often began with making a packing list, only to find myself distracted by other chores. My mother, on the other hand, was meticulous and began preparing her suitcase well in advance, purchasing essentials and neatly arranging them to leave room for more.

The story then transitions to Maundy Thursday and the Last Supper, a testament to Leonardo da Vinci's talent. The scene portrays Jesus with his twelve disciples gathered around a spread of bread and wine, though the exact details of their meal remain a mystery. Traditionally, Christian households served rice cake and a drink on Maundy Thursday, and Mummyamma, my maternal grandmother, prepared the table for the occasion.

This table, made of lovely rosewood and seating eight, held a special place in the family. In the past, it had served as a study table for Amma and her two brothers. Siblings sat on either side of Amma, and any crossing of boundaries, even by the tiniest object, often led to squabbles.

Mummyamma's table featured rice cakes and drinks for the Maundy Thursday tradition. Family members would gather and recite a prayer, and the eldest member would cut the cake.

Traditionally, the rice cake would be equally divided among the family members, but on this particular night, we substituted buns instead.

With two hours remaining before our departure for the airport, all was going well until a glass of drink crashed to the floor from someone's hands. According to old grandmother tales, this was a bad omen, possibly a story concocted by a mother who cherished her crockery collection. If that was the case, she had indeed succeeded in keeping her clumsy child's hands off her precious items. We cleaned up the mess and continued, but a sense of lethargy and drowsiness overcame me, for it was well past my bedtime.

Despite my fatigue, the excitement of the trip kept me alert. Could the glass have been responsible for our predicament? I pondered this question as I watched Amma from a distance. Blaming an everyday object for our mistake didn't seem right. I couldn't hear their conversation, but it didn't seem like we would be travelling that day. How much worse could this Good Friday possibly get?

CHAPTER 2

The counter staff was back to attending to the rest of the people in the queue. Everybody got back to business. The crowd thickened in no time as many more travellers arrived. Some moved about with bulging suitcases while a few others thrust stubborn trolleys. What made the wait fun was observing these people that I would probably never meet in my life again, being their real selves, and when people are oblivious to everyone around them, it is entertaining to watch. In a crowd like this, you will see all sorts of people. All sorts. The overdressed, the underdressed, the overprepared, the underprepared, and a few other interesting individuals that you and I would not normally meet in our boring everyday lives. This kept me busy for a good while until we were called again.

Fate was not completely callous. It had opened not one but two equally impractical choices. The first choice drew out any hope there was left to travel. And as for the second choice, with the prices of the tickets changing every other minute and with the banks on leave, it was also not workable as suggested by the mystery man. We got ready to leave. Around a quarter past midnight, an airport taxi took us back. Home was another two hours away, and on our way, I sat thinking if we would ever travel to Europe that vacation. It was difficult to imagine myself and the rest of us in Europe again after all that happened.

I remember waking to silence the following morning only to see everybody unusually quiet with a gadget each in front checking for tickets. "This one is all booked," said Papa. "So is this!" said Amma. We would call different agencies, but all of them had the same disappointing reply. "We will call you back," some would say. But the phone never rang. When no more hope was found through phone calls, my parents left to see what was possible. By this time, most of my clothes and other contents of my luggage were already on their respective shelves.

I began to think about the previous day when I was all excited and looking forward to the trip. But only if I and the rest of us had known what awaited us was sheer disappointment! They returned after two hours with the news that we would be flying in business class on the same day as all the other tickets were booked. Before they even completed it, I found myself packing the luggage again. Had I waited for two more hours, I could have avoided this trouble. But then my mind was once again at work, thinking of the good time I would soon have.

The airport lights were there, welcoming us once again. A different lady sat at the counter, and as for the mystery man, he was nowhere to be seen. Men, women, and children propelled suitcases of different fun colours and sizes. The lounge's door opened to a dimly lit room with puffy satin couches placed in the centre. Soft instrumental music (of a harpist) played in the background, which created a peaceful ambience overall. We walked into the lounge to witness important people with plenty of deadlines up front sitting before their laptops. There were some who were seated next to the buffet counter, where a strong aroma bobbed up. The staff is always a bit partial to passengers travelling in business class (unless the first-class passengers are present) and would let you board the plane before anyone else.

It can be endless when counting the benefits of travelling in business class. There were specially designed seats that could be adjusted to one's comfort so that the regular wriggling and twisting of bodies into uncomfortable positions were not required. A confined space so that nobody interrupts your alone time. One call, and you have whatever dish you desire on the table in front of you. Anyone would begrudge even a day of such supremacy. The air smelled luxurious, and so did the interior, but the people did not seem quite so interesting except for the couple who sat in front.

I knew they were British because they spoke English with a heavy British accent. Both of them were very polite and would occasionally smile at everyone on board. In the four-hour flight to Abu Dhabi, they managed to down six to seven generous glasses of champagne (probably why they were more fun than the rest of us on board) while their daughter sat close by, singing sweetly to a doll-like child (cut to the future: it turns out it really was a doll and not an actual child). The only colour came from our clothes; the rest were in the monochromatic shades of grey and black, coming from the spotless "only dry clean" blazers of serious-looking men and women.

We reached Abu Dhabi around noon, and from there, it was another long flight to Manchester. Anoop (Amma's younger brother) came to pick us up. He looked different. It was probably the way he walked or maybe a good few inches he had grown since our last reunion (I am well aware of the fact that men don't grow in size after a certain age, but there was something different about him). He had changed.

My first impression of the city is still vivid. Tall buildings, traffic-free and trash-free roads. When I say buildings, they were not just any tall buildings in similar tones that were common and boring. They were buildings with remarkable details that drew attention. That was Manchester. The city that is known for its brilliant architecture.

EASTER

Christmas has cookies, the exchanging of presents, and blinding ornaments hanging from trees. Easter has Easter eggs and… well, Easter eggs. The day, of course, is so much more than breaking the fast and celebrating; it is looked forward to after a lot of preparation. Firstly, there is Lent. Then come the many preparations taken by churches, and finally, after 50 days of sacrifice and building faith, the fast is broken.

An Easter morning in most Christian households starts early when everybody gets ready for the holy mass with an empty stomach. Half an hour into the mass, one can hear the stomachs grumbling and roaring, pleading for food, and from there, one begins to lose focus on the sermons being preached. After the mass, the older generation is usually seen chatting and catching up on neighbourhood news, and that is also usually around when questions like "Who is this?" and "What do they do?" directed at us, surface from amiable-looking faces creased with wrinkles. The breakfast that follows the mass is what everybody looks forward to. Easter repasts are usually grand to make up for the days that one would have to go without including meat in their diet. In my memory, there has not been a feast that has been broken without Mummyamma's signature mutton curry.

CHAPTER 3

The neighbourhood church was a small one. No gaudy ornamentation except for the minuscule cross that stood well above. Anyone who is not a regular visitor of the church would have a hard time spotting it for at least the next couple of minutes, for it was well hidden among the canopy of a few shady trees. We could faintly hear the hymns that came from a distance. There were a few English families that stood reciting rosaries. Apart from them, the church seemed pretty much empty. I always liked the idea of a simple church with an interior free from shiny distractions, and this was often difficult to find in the place I came from because of the myriad of churches that were built to accommodate many. It had wooden benches for seating and a few images painted on the glasses right below its ceiling. The daily prayers were recited, the scripture readings were completed, and peace was exchanged, followed by the celebration of the Eucharist. Although this celebration is a predominant part of every holy mass, it was only that day I learned that the method of the distribution of the bread and wine varied.

The priest distributed the bread; however, the red wine was kept separately, open to all those who wished a sip from the gold-plated ciborium. "The body of Christ!" proclaimed the priest, extending his hand to place it in my mouth. The bread dissolved in my mouth in no time, but I debated about taking a sip of the wine. I watched how it was done. "It can't be that hard," I told myself while walking towards the pastor holding the wine glass. To his surprise and to everyone else's, I showed no hesitation in taking the ciborium in my hand and sipping a little more than what was normally given. People looked confused. Was I not supposed to do it? Apparently, everybody who went before me had faked drinking from the cup, as only a little was left, and the only way of getting even a tiny sip was by tilting the cup like how I did.

There was little surprise when my brother, like always, never missed an opportunity to poke fun at me. So, on our way back home, the narration of what took place minutes ago was done. The addition of his own share of humour to what had actually happened made everyone laugh, which would not have been possible if only what had actually happened was told. "*Maybe it wasn't that bad after all,*" I thought to myself when everyone else had a good laugh at my expense. But this was only because I knew Mummyamma's mutton curry awaited me in the kitchen.

There was no problem that her mutton curry could not fix. It is a green curry with a thick consistency that calls for a secret ingredient left to soak the previous night. It is then ground to a thick paste, which is later used for marinating the mutton along with the other ingredients and is usually served in a bowl beside Ammachi's (my paternal grandmother's) cutlets. What usually followed after breakfast was a game of Bluff. Like the name, the game, in its most basic sense, revolved around telling lies, and anyone who won the game was seen as a liar. It gets a bit tricky here; although lying is not considered foul, anything apart from it is not entertained in the game. This includes peeping into the other person's cards or hiding them when nobody is watching. A very interesting game, I must say… something that promotes a bad habit while still allowing one to keep their morals. My cousins and I would sit in a circle (sometimes accompanied by Appachan) to play.

The game could go on for between thirty minutes to one hour and usually end with Ajay winning the game (liar). The sun shined brightly, producing a lovely picnic spot in the narrow lane in front of my uncles's and aunty's lovely little home. The weather was more than free from fault for a game of Bluff. It went on for more than one hour (the longest we had ever played). After a few minutes and a couple of games later, the game ended with Appachan once again losing to Ajay. Appachan was alright and was even ready to be defeated again after having his share of the piping hot biriyani. The park was a few crosses down the road, but we went by car as we were the kind of people who would take transportation to the park and back and would walk only a little distance along its perimeter. The car went down the road and eventually made headway to the garden at the end of the street. The sunlight fell on the branches in bloom, but no change was brought to the atmosphere (cold winds were still cold). Winds blew, the branches swayed, and the sickly-sweet fragrance of the foreign flowers interrupted daily walks. Dogs of various breeds fetched sticks while they were still on leash. Afraid of dog scratches, we moved to an open ground with ample space.

"This seems more than fine. Cold breeze, fresh air, and no dogs," said Appachan, heaving a sigh of relief. But just in time, a dog came, happily flapping its ears at the mention of it. Dawn broke across my face. What more could I ask for? A dog happy to see me? I can confirm that it was the first time it had happened. They would usually follow my brother. There was something about my brother that drew them to him, not to mention he also had a knack for handling them. The names of these dogs were quite different from the ones that one would normally hear. There was a Beagle named Bentley and another dog of a breed that I was not familiar with named Freckles because of the many spots it had on its back. There were many more of different kinds. The park looked pretty, with light falling on every blossomed flower in its way. We decided to stop for the day when the cold breeze still continued, making it difficult for any further exploration. In the three days that followed, nothing much was done apart from the trips made to the convenience stores.

Anything that hinted at running out of pantry goods would leave my uncle no option but to take Alan (my toddler cousin) and me to the nearby store. Initially, we had them convinced that the only purpose of visiting these stores was to help them pick out the required items, but after a couple of trips later, they understood our hidden agenda was to shop for candies. We were sent out on only one condition, and that was to obey their orders of covering ourselves up from head to toe. They said that they did not want us to spoil the rest of the vacation by being down with a cold, so we covered ourselves with mittens, sweaters, and gloves. In the end, we always looked unrecognisable, to say the least. It was seldom that we could see what was on our way because of everything that was wrapped around us. That is how I spent the first few days in Manchester. The rest, unlike us, would find pleasure in any kind of work. This gradually made it into the routine for the next couple of days till my father joined us.

My uncle celebrated Papa's arrival on the 17th with another drive to the park with Appachan. Some of the adults initiated the purchase of cardigans along with gloves, while the rest were engaged in other tasks. The weather forecast showed a possibility of a mild downpour, so a final drive to the store was made. Our suitcases were once again out, confectioneries were prepared, and hampers made. It was ensured that the chores were distributed equally to prevent any disagreement or delays. My brother and I had to load the luggage, and confectioneries were prepared by all the mothers. Appachan supervised the preparations, and my uncle, who was the only international licence holder among us, had to drive. Alan was exempted from doing anything and was strictly instructed not to cause trouble. The day that we planned to start our travel had finally arrived after a long wait of three days. We loaded the luggage. It was not as easy as it sounded and should not be taken lightly. The suitcases went in the back. Hampers and anything edible went in the front, which was within our reach. The other things that required their own individual places were given special allotments. The car we booked had arrived a day prior to the trip. It was a black Mercedes, a ten-seater.

CHAPTER 4

The thought of a serene countryside existing in a country with more than one sprawling city seemed quite surreal until we visited the Lake District. The long roads of Lakeland stood, wedged by seemingly endless houses enclosed with cobbled walls. The car swerved in unexpected directions, moving past more green fields, and in these green fields were sheep. They stood grazing in the open space like white fuzzy balls when viewed from a good distance, unaware of the danger that surrounded them in the form of hungry foxes. All these sheep reminded me of a good old one called Dolly. She was from Scotland and was famous worldwide as she was the first mammal cloned from an adult cell. Unlike the rest of the sheep that moved about, she was unlucky as she had to spend her entire life in a closed space under the supervision of many people. How difficult it must have been for her to stay away from such alluring green fields with plenty of fresh grass to feed on? In a way, it was better to stay well-fed and famous than to end up as a roast at some farmer's dinner table. The sheep, left free, wandered aimlessly. There were plenty. Most of them stood drooling over the few strands of grass that outgrew the others while the rest dozed off, their swollen feet unable to bear the weight of their heavily swollen torsos.

We waited till they cleared our path. This sort of waiting was not new to us. The only thing was that it was not sheep that blocked the roads back in India. It was cows. They would gracefully lie munching on plastic trash, and whatever other objects they found appetising to feed on, and when honked at, they would look at you. They would either take their sweet little time to clear their way (if you got lucky) or would stir a little and continue resting. When that happens, you will have to diligently move without hurting the innocent creature. It was just sheep and vacant plots for hours on end. The buildings we passed by looked empty. We went a little further down that road, and I can say that our complaints were resolved to some extent. Smoke bobbed up from cobbled hearths, and occasionally, salt and pepper heads peeked out to make sure that their sheep were safe and that no foxes got away with them.

Lush green fields and towering trees. Willows and birch. Cypress and oaks. The scenery had switched to more mountain silhouettes and streams, but this time, the number of sheep that could be spotted had reduced considerably. "Turn left," came a voice directing us, tuning out whatever distractions could be heard in the background. It was from one of the mobiles that helped us get to Windermere. A few lefts, a few rights, further down the road and up. We had reached The Windermere Boat Jetty Museum. It was a building on stilts with water underneath. The museum displayed a wide variety of boats. There were different coloured boats on the floor with railings lifting them away from the surface, and a few wooden paddle boats hung on the wall. Our real purpose of visiting Windermere was to be somewhere else. The clouds turned a dull shade of blue, indicating a mild shower like the weather forecast suggested. It looked like the clouds would burst any second.

The outlines of the defaced bricks, indistinguishable with the passage of time, led to an English cottage far away from everything. The wild bushes muffled the noisy world beyond. On a day like this, the lake poets (William Wordsworth and his counterpart Samuel Taylor Coleridge) were halted at the same house that stood before us: The Dove Cottage. The cosy cottage front, embossed with ferns and mosses, was only a few paces away, but it was never the same. The house was under renovation. William and his sister, Dorothy, were joined by the extended Wordsworth family in this house. All our expectations dialled down as our craned necks made an attempt to see the changes that were being made. "Bad luck had its way this time," I said while moving the few splinters of wood from the renovation to the side. The old bay window that protruded might be from where young William looked through, watching the distant hills and lakes from the warmth of his cottage. We walked further down the village compound where young Wordsworth once walked. The hypnotic charm of the beautiful surroundings told us why anyone would be tempted to write poems after experiencing such magnetism. William and Dorothy would often go for nature walks. One such walk inspired one of his most recognisable works: The Daffodils.

"When we were in the woods beyond Gowbarrow Park, we saw a few daffodils close to the waterside. But as we went along, there were more and yet more, and at last, under the boughs of the trees, we saw that there was a long belt of them along the shore, about the breadth of a country turnpike road. I never saw daffodils so beautiful. They grew about the mossy stones, some rested their heads upon these stones as on a pillow for weariness, and the rest tossed and reeled and danced and seemed as if they were verily laughing with the wind that blew upon them over the lake."

– Grasmere Journal.

It is bizarre how a few ignored daffodils that surfaced from some dampened stone caught anyone's eyes, let alone a poet's. When I later pondered about the same, it occurred to me that sometimes it is people like them who notice what usually goes unnoticed. I remember learning the poem a year ago in eighth grade.

I wandered lonely as a cloud
That floats on high o'er vales and hills,
When all at once I saw a crowd,
A host, of golden daffodils;
Beside the lake, beneath the trees,
Fluttering and dancing in the breeze.

– Daffodils

I mouthed, not able to recall the rest. From Dorothy's memoirs (The Grasmere Journals), it was obvious how their little house was something more than just a simple abode. Unlike William's poems with optimistic endings, the poet had to move to a different lodging, leaving the cottage where he had made beautiful memories. There, in that house, he spent the fag end of his life singing lullabies to his children and writing poems up until he died in 1850. A cottage on the crest of the hills seemed grand and luxurious, but I am sure that this cottage, tucked behind a few wild bushes, held a special place in the siblings' hearts. There was a souvenir shop a few paces down. There, we found The Dove Cottage embossed on objects of all bizarre shapes and forms and daffodils painted on porcelain plates. Wordsworth and his family were buried in St Oswald's Church, a few miles from the cottage. The roads were wet from the rain. It got heavier as we got to the church. We still visited the tomb despite the poor weather conditions because it would have been a shame not to see it after having travelled so far. The tomb was difficult to find, as it was just one among many— one among the tombs of ordinary men. Out in the rain and blistering heat, it stood with the letters engraved upon it that read:

WILLIAM WORDSWORTH 1850
MARY WORDSWORTH 1859

Nothing more, nothing less. No adornments or anything fancy for that matter. In the time we took to explore the place, my uncle had disappeared. He said he was going to get something, but we did not know what it was. When we got into the car, it smelled of something freshly baked—not a cake or anything we could immediately identify. Guesses were made, but eventually, everyone gave up. What was that object giving off such a strong scent? Only my uncle knew. Without making us wait much longer, he pulled out a few square pieces of a snack covered in greasy parchment that had been folded multiple times

"Remember, anyone?"

Of course! The Grasmere Gingerbread!" I exclaimed, bells ringing in my head. Grasmere is not only known for its brilliant writers; it attracts tourists from around the world by offering some of the best gingerbread anyone can imagine.

This famous shop (The Grasmere Gingerbread) lies close to the churchyard and even shares its border with the old cottage (now renovated into the café). It was started in 1854 by a Victorian cook named Sarah Nelson. Today, there is not a single soul who leaves Grasmere without tasting this delicacy. Gingerbread, with its closest parallel being regular bread, is infused with more than eight different spices. When dipped in the flavorful rum butter, it delivers a delightful kick.

"Run, run as fast as you can. You cannot catch me because I am the gingerbread man!" Amma added to the elation.

My mind travelled back at once to my toddler days, when I was put to sleep by my father's brilliant narrations. Red Riding Hood and Gingerbread Man—my two favourite picks back then—were often read to me after I was tucked into bed.

"It is funny how kids shoot up," said Papa. I remember listening to his narration. He would read the first few pages of the book and stop at the cliffhanger. This was to help my brother and I develop a liking for reading (and it worked).

Upon Alan's (my toddler cousin) request, all the windows were rolled up because he did not want his freshly baked gingerbread to run away from him like what happened in the book.

"Hmmmmm." I tightly gripped onto mine because I definitely did not want it to flee away from us, at least not after bringing water into our mouths.

The gingerbread and the butterbeer disappeared into our tummies, leaving only a few flakes on the parchment. "One… two… three…" I counted till Ajay interrupted. I was counting the number of rivers that we passed by.

"That river there. Is it not from Harry Potter?" he asked while pointing to a river that resembled Loch Shiel in structure. It sure did look like it.

"Harry Potter?" asked Appachan, confused.

"Is he not that child who fought the noseless hooligan?"

"Yep! That is him," I said.

SCOTLAND

The summer months of April and May in Scotland are relatively said to be the best travel time. It is when the shy buds of spring flowers bloom, and the gleaming waters flow, teeming with life. The temperature can go down to twenty degrees or below, so one must be prepared to experience even awfully cold winters. The trip was interrupted by stops made at every convenience store. The shelves would sometimes contain nothing after the elevenses. However, whatever was left would be arranged well and stacked on top of one another until it was restocked. We made such stops every time to stretch our legs and freshen up. Because of these stops, it took us longer to get to Scotland. The sun disappeared behind the clouds. We could now see the outline of the Scottish Highlands. When coming closer, the trees very strangely reminded me of the greens that most children dreaded. Tall, bushy trees looked like boiled broccoli, and the fine leaves of the willow trees looked identical to shredded pieces of water spinach. It was past dusk. Fog blurred our vision, and in the distance, my ears could roughly grasp the cries of seagulls. The drive was dangerous as the roads were slippery. We were getting closer to the home of one of the most gigantic fictional beasts, the Lochness Monster, popularly known among children as Nessie. Beneath the dark blue waters of Loch Ness hides a monster. With a huge lump but smooth, it cannot be distinguished from an enormous eel, but the truth only the witnesses know.

"Don't those mountains look like they can easily hide something as big as a monster?" I asked.

"Who knows! There might be one or two hiding behind!" Ajay said, joining in on the fun. A few miles from the city and the lady spoke again.

"You have arrived at your destination," she said.

We could not have been more confused. We ruled out the possibility of each of the buildings being our hostel one by one. The pictures that we saw were quite different from the building that stood in front of us. But we decided that whichever building suited the picture the most was our building. The car turned back to the city in search of restaurants. Picking restaurants had to be the easiest of everything we had to do while travelling with a bunch of people of different age groups. Even though our personal preferences varied, we stuck to one cuisine: Indian. The sudden blow of the Scottish wind as soon as I planted my feet on the ground left me breathless. The temperature touched eleven degrees, the coldest that we had ever experienced. I am sure that night was like any other night for Scotland's people, but it was nowhere close to the climate that we were brought up in. The Indian climate is said to be more of a monsoon type. Strong winds would blow, and along with this would sometimes come the juicy mangoes from your neighbouring orchard. For us, we have the Himalayan mountains to the north that obstruct the icy cold winds blowing from Central Asia and the warm summers that trigger melanin production, giving us the warm, swarthy complexion that we are proud of. The wind stung my body. My teeth chattered as fog escaped my mouth and condensed in the cold air. Though shivering, I managed to get inside the restaurant. The air that managed to sweep in along with me did not disturb the diners, but the Indian curries that were not meant for their spice tolerance did. Hindi records played from the gramophone in the background. The walls were adorned with Mithila Art, and the strong scent of lit incense sticks made it seem like any family dinner that we had back home.

The lady kept showing us the same destination, and our car kept going around the roundabout. The night never seemed to end. We decided to recheck our directions. Out came a wrinkled piece of paper from Appachan's pocket. Yes, he had written it down on paper because he, unlike us, did not trust technology. He says that it is a lot easier this way. In bold, curly handwriting that stood slanting was the address: 413 Glimerton Road EH177JJ, Edinburgh. "She did not mean that building," said Appachan, pointing to a building that seemed to show absolutely no sign of activity. "Yes, looks about right," said my uncle. He was in charge of the accommodation and transportation departments, both of which he managed to get done exceptionally well.

"So it was this house that we were looking for all this while?" I asked, watching the building that was painfully visible from the roadside. A few branches creaked as the winds still blew. Nobody answered the door despite the gentle knocks that were being made on it. The door screeched open to a narrow passageway with doors on either side. The walls stood exhibiting framed pictures of the different architectural wonders of every country in existence. A chandelier hung above the kitchenette, and pots and pans of shining silver were enclosed in transparent cabinets. The rooms were well-curtained with floral prints on them. These rooms, with barely any furnishing, still looked warm. The respective rooms were chosen, and everybody dispersed for the night. Our hostel mates were seen on rare occasions. There were two of them that we got a glimpse of a tall brunette with a smiling face and a charming lad with blonde tresses. We saw them only when the weather conditions were bad and left them confined to the hostel rooms.

EDINBURG CASTLE

The castle sits on the crest of a massive castle rock surrounded by trees. It dates back to the 1100s and is the oldest building in Scotland. It was built by King David for his devoted mother, Saint Margaret of Scotland, and therefore epitomises the bond between a mother and her son. Many of Scotland's renowned writers, soldiers, and noblemen were laid to rest in the graveyard down below (the Greyfriars Kirkyard). It is from here that JK Rowling is said to have gotten inspiration for some of the names of her characters, like Thomas Riddle, who was later adapted as Tom Riddle in the books. From the graveyard is a flight of stairs connecting to the castle ground. The steps never seemed to end as we made an effort to get to the top. Surprisingly, Appachan, who had reached there before any of us, had already started the walking tour. The castle greeted us with its gaping doorway that was once the pathway of Scottish kings and queens. The colossal gates with rusted bolts that were once open to only the royals were now open to all. A few paces from there stood hordes of tourists, all carried away by the enchanting view from the castle. The dusky shades of the evening sky made a decent background for the silhouetting buildings that stood in the heart of the city.

A sudden explosive noise startled me. The sound was only a little worse than a confetti cannon popped on birthdays. I was not able to recall reading anything about it. I looked around to see where it was from. It was from a cannon—a black object with a protruding pipe that is fired to help navigate ships. The booklet that I read did not mention anything about the firing of cannons. It is fired around 1:00 PM every day except Sundays in the northern part of the castle. The rustic stone-strewn walls featured a wall bedecked with autographs of Queen Elizabeth, all framed and nailed to the wall, leaving uniform spaces. The museum also exhibited medals, weapons, war debris, and uniforms of brave Scottish soldiers who died on the battleground. The light drizzles and the wild winds didn't stop Appachan's enthusiastic self from exploring. "This should do," he said, covering his bald head with a spare handkerchief.

We decided on a meeting spot and separated into two groups. The group that opted for further exploration headed west, while the other group headed the polar opposite. The vibrant souvenir store that displayed postcards stood out from the rest, probably because the other stores didn't have anything of my interest. There were postcards of the castle and other famous Scottish monuments and structures on rotating racks. Woollen mittens were next. There were a variety of them. Colourful ones. The less interesting ones and some, although essentially obtained from the same animal, somehow provided more warmth. Then, there were several stalls of expensive pashmina, all set up together in a confusing bundle away from the entrance. I moved out to wait on a bench for the others after I managed to choose from the many options. Opposite where we rested, restless toddlers ran on a hunt for castle treasures while their parents sat helplessly. Much to their misery, the guide never stopped speaking of the swords that the kings might have left behind, along with the treasure, building more exhilaration in them. I kept running into more interesting people as I continued the tour on foot until I saw an overflowing crowd before me. They were all moving towards the direction from where a strange but mysterious music played. The sound grew recognisable as we walked towards a Scottish gentleman in a kilt (a traditional Scottish dress worn by men) playing the bagpipes.

"A very Scottish something to witness while we are here," said Papa. The gentleman moved his head happily as he played the instrument. I am sure he was as hypnotised by the musical notes as much as the audience who cheered him on. Appachan scrutinised the instrument for a minute or two, turned back, and asked,

"Heard of the story of bagpipes?"

I threw my mind back. But then again, there wasn't anything I could recall. I allowed my grandfather to narrate. Nobody ever questioned Appachan's ability to narrate.

For the voracious reader that he was, he was able to come up with a story for everything around him (the sky being the limit). He cleared his throat the usual way before any narration. "It draws people's attention," he says. "This folktale begins from a small town where the population of humans was surpassed by that of rodents."

Every detail, except the end, was the same. The story felt familiar, but being the good listener I was, I listened carefully. Interrupting his flow of narration would be disrespectful, so I nodded my head every time there was a pause or a sudden rise in volume. "The mayor announced a large amount as a reward for the person who could put an end to the problem . The next day, a man in a strange disguise showed up, promising to drive away all the mice. He took out an instrument and started playing a strange tune," he continued. I listened patiently until... "When the pied piper was given only half of what was promised, he played the strange tune once again. But this time, instead of the rodents, children followed until they were locked up in a faraway cave. Their parents followed them as well, hoping that the pied piper would let them out, but he didn't. The parents knelt down, thumbing the beads of their rosary, till a blinding light appeared in the skies that demanded their kids be freed, and that... is the story of bagpipes," he said, with his lips wanting to break into a chuckle. This wasn't the ending. Appachan knew it just as well as I did.

"It probably was a different interpretation," I thought. A religious one, perhaps? Walking further down, there were more stalls with more cards, magnets, and souvenirs. The weather grew wild. The trees swayed, and the leaves rustled.

THE FORTH BRIDGE

It was our last day in Scotland. We drove the car to the Forth Bridge and parked on land not far away from the bridge, a place from where the bridge was visible. Ripples formed like the ones that normally form when hurling stones at the water, but this was formed due to the wind. It moved beneath the bridge that stood in front of us: The Forth Bridge. Its structure caused awe and raised many questions. How anybody could construct such a complex structure remained a mystery. This UNESCO World Heritage site stands even today as a symbol of Scotland. Beside this bridge ran another bridge: The Queensferry Crossing.

CHAPTER 5

GLASGOW

To every Glaswegian (Glasgow's people), this city remains a port city where the export of goods was the common trade. The cargoes would depart Clyde, laden with farm essentials and other fundamentals that would be exported. But those days are long gone. Today, Glasgow is an industrialised city in the West Central Lowlands of Scotland. 42 miles away from Edinburgh, this city took us about two hours to reach. Every time I sat idle in a car, jetlag would pay me a visit, or *was it just because of sheer exhaustion from the hectic travel schedule?* I wondered while being extremely drowsy. The next time I was awake, I was in front of the Glasgow Cathedral. This church, otherwise identified as the Church of St. Mungo, was dedicated to Glasgow's founder, St Mungo. He was recognised not only as the patron saint of Glasgow but also for the miracles he performed during his early life. On visiting Glasgow, an emblem was frequently seen. At first glance, the emblem looked like any other crest that was seen etched onto the buildings, but little does one realise the stories behind it. The four predominant miracles performed by St Mungo were brought together in this emblem, generally monikered as The Coat of Arms of Glasgow.

> Here is the bird that never flew
> Here is the tree that never grew
> Here is the bell that never rang
> Here is the fish that never swam

The relics of St Mungo are buried on the cathedral ground. Its mint green roof stood out from the rustic brown that covered the church's exterior. Vibrant colours stood out from the stained-glass pieces. When reflecting light, it would be an exemplary representation of the symmetrical patterns like that of a kaleidoscope. The cavernous hall of the cathedral had vaulted ceilings. All rustic and ancient, of course! The track lights that were fitted between the church's arched structures highlighted the gothic architecture. "It was here I parked," said my uncle, shocked by the sudden disappearance of the car. Walking further he asked, "Or was it here?" His eyes were still searching for signs. When the car was finally found on the street two blocks away, we drove to the hotel where we were planning to spend the night. "Could we please see the rooms?" asked Amma, hoping for a positive answer.

Kind enough, the lady came with us, unlike most receptionists who would direct you to your rooms. Up we climbed the few flights of stairs, taking every right and left she took until we faced a wooden door fitted with a golden plaque that read 13G. All the plenteous furniture had a place in the crammed room. Behind the door was a neatly made bed. Even a shabby fold or line would have been difficult to find. Next to the bed were two armchairs ornamented with designs and patterns of all sorts, and the curtains in murky shades of blue and black made the room appear darker than it already was. No sentences, complex or simple, could convince my claustrophobic grandfather about spending a night there. He quickly scanned the corners and turned away, expressing discomfort at the very thought of spending a night. The receptionist, still positive about us confirming the booking, turned to us, and her pleasant smile began to appear. She continued to show us around the other facilities the building had to offer. The antiquity of the kitchen reminded me of the cathedral we visited just a short while ago. The cafeteria and the kitchen were partitioned by a curry-stained curtain and a bare shelf. The conclusion we came to saddened both (the lady and us). To make up for the days, we went by without travelling; the elders agreed to take us on every shopping trip possible. It was through these shopping trips that we discovered that the practice of selling venison wasn't, in fact, illegal. I also learnt about a few other things (like the existence of the car boot sale) through these trips. Who knew that shopping in those local stores would have been this unpredictably informative?!

CHAPTER 6

I remember that the first time I heard of Roman Baths, what came into my mind were debris and ruins, but I was not all right. Sure! It is known for its ancient bathhouse and ruins, but it has a side that is less known to the public. The Roman fortified land had streets thickly packed with luxury brands. Throngs sauntered past, and among them were a few desiring the shiny clothes that covered the mannequins. Young girls stood admiring the models that featured on the opaque designer doors. And an exuberant group of a few stood fascinated by the acts done by the street performers. On the right, pianists were seen seated on bench-like chairs, their fingers moving almost flawlessly while playing the notes. A little further, magicians (who were equally surprised as us to see how the rabbits hopped off from their hats, which they wore not more than a while ago) were seen performing their magical acts. They wore black satin capes with red lining. As for their foreheads, they were free from any remarkable scars. Turning around, we saw a few daring people jumping from pole to pole.

I stood in a place where I could watch both the acts and the tourists getting their tickets punched. I could see that the queue was getting longer. As we entered, we were given mini walkie-talkie-like objects. These, I believe, were used to substitute the need for a guide. The little object had dial pads which, when clicked, would educate you on anything that piqued your curiosity. Each place or artefact is numbered, and when that number is pressed, you learn a little bit about how it came into being, how it was used, and what it is made from. What makes the Roman Bath special is its hot water stream, which contains many minerals that come from deep down the Earth's surface. During the ancient times when the bath was used, Roman lead pipes (the then popular plumbing material) were deployed to transport this rich water to the main bath. The use of lead pipes was later switched to clay pipes after it was found that the toxins present in lead were the cause of poisoning among many Romans.

Legend has it that it was only after a certain incident that people started acknowledging its existence. According to it, the founder of this magical water stream was a king named Baldud (a figure hailing from the old folk tales of Britain). His statue was placed somewhere that easily caught everybody's attention. The paint had faded and was even flaking off. He had a walrus moustache covering his upper lip and had eyes that were round and prominent. In the beginning, the Roman Bath and its miracle-working streams weren't given any importance. When stories spread about how the king had fallen prey to leprosy, his people forced him out of town. With nowhere to go and nothing to do, he roamed around aimlessly, eventually ending up at a pigsty. There, he took care of the pigs till the disease spread to them. The pigs would often go to a hot, muddy pool nearby and roll themselves in it. This, although it was only a natural tendency for any pig, cured the disease. Shocked by the results, even the king started bathing in the hot water stream and was soon healed. Many believed this incident to be a miracle by the Sulis Goddess (the goddess of healing water), and because Goddess Minerva, the Roman goddess of wisdom, was considered no different from the Sulis Goddess, people began to call her Sulis Minerva (a name that is a combination of the two). The hot water spring is still something that convinces people (only a minority) to believe in the power of the thermal goddess Sulis Minerva.

It is possible that the water we now see gushing out of the Roman channels was only raindrops when they first fell on the Mendip Hills. This passageway ran through the limestones beneath the bath. As thanks to the goddess, they built a shrine for her inside a temple next to the bath. In this temple, the priests made sacrifices to the goddess, either requesting help to win battles or pleading to punish people for their wrongdoings. Those were the times when bathing was considered a huge deal, unlike now. People would bathe twice and thrice, and if presented with more water, then several more times.

If bathing were as exciting as it was then, even we would be motivated to spend such long hours to thoroughly clean ourselves. They had an organised routine. It would start with them warming up their bodies by exercising to make the rest of the process easier. The sweating body is warmed again in the tepidarium. Soaps weren't used then; instead, scented oils (kept in mini flasks) were applied all over the body and would be later scraped off using a strigil (a wooden tool designed for this purpose). The caldarium (being the hottest) was used next for the steam, followed by the frigidarium (the cold room). The Roman Bath was also seen as a site for socialising. People would gather there to talk and discuss matters. The idea of communal bathing, however, was criticised by many. In the second century, the then-ruling emperor imposed a law forbidding both genders to bathe in public. The building was then reconstructed, allowing both men and women to take baths separately. As we passed by the rooms, we saw animated videos projected onto walls for a better understanding of how the bath might have looked during those days, as today, some rooms contain only ruins. The room where the tepidarium stood only had the hypocaust, showing how the floors were heated then. At first, it looked like only blocks of bricks (which it was) built here and there, almost as though the construction was stopped midway through the making of something important. The Museum of Bath exhibited some of the archaeological findings and artefacts. With plenty of questions in my head, I moved towards the mysterious findings older than anybody in the room. Minerva's golden head was one of the things that were displayed, and one thing that would have made it into the exhibiting shelf without much doubt was Appachan's almost obsolete mobile phone. People who saw this thought there was no better way to stay connected with our ancient history than that. "All of this is too complicated," would be the reply given to anyone who questioned why Appachan still sticks to old technology.

Then, the shelves exhibited pallets with something written on them. These could have been the pallets containing curses. These were complaints to punish people for whatever they were caught guilty of, whether it was stealing or any other act, big or small. There were also a few gemstones enclosed in glass cases that were once a part of the rings worn by the visitors who often visited the Roman Baths. Some believe that those stones, which were once a part of the rings they wore, lost their adhesive because they would wear them in the water.

While making our way to the spring overflow, someone caught my eye. She was aged but vivacious. The veil that was carelessly wrapped around her neck fell as she looked down to knit. This was to show how some of the visitors would have spent their time before or after they got in the bath. There was a fountain close to the exit. Its floor shone with the coins that were thrown into it. These were thrown in by people to make a wish, and it would have taken forever to count them all. Not knowing if these wishes were granted, we walked to the exit. People crowded there to taste the spa water that is said to be rich in numerous minerals. In a way, we were lucky because before, visitors had to pay for the water that tasted awful. Forgetting about the walkie-talkie resting in our bags, we made our way out when the loud noise of the metal-detecting machine went off. But we were just in time for some street performance. What we saw as soon as we got out was a man who stood on a pole eight feet from the ground doing stunts. The streets were full of daring performers like him, and that itself was entertaining to watch. For a good distance, the street was packed with people and had smaller paths leading to more street performances.

STONEHENGE

We couldn't help but stop near the yellow mustard flower beds. They were moving gently in unison along with the breeze, making it look like a wave of yellow. Boards stood in clear, bold letters threatening a huge sum of penalty to those who stopped by the road. The visually appealing fields were just as hard to discard as the signboard that stood glaring at us. The only space that didn't show any such signboard was close to a village road that had a sparkling stream flowing by.

All of us got out of the car, noticing a building which we assumed to be the visitor's centre. It had everything to keep its visitors engaged. There was a café to help visitors fuel up, a powder room, a washroom, and an open ground with tables on which artefacts and a bunch of other sharp tools (which scared children) were kept. What more could a visitor possibly ask for? People formed lines after the bus engine roared to life. The bus was empty, which could possibly mean that the others preferred to walk. As the bus moved past the green grounds, we were able to see the scornful people who made the great decision to walk on an ice-cold day. Alan slightly turned his head to the window with his tongue sticking out, enjoying the breeze that messed with his hair. The sun showed up, making everything around look surreal. The marvellous stone structure stood in the middle of... a ground... It is inexplicable as to how the stones got in the middle of nowhere. The origins of Stonehenge remain a mystery that ended with its creators. Stonehenge and its surroundings were added to the UNESCO World Heritage site in 1986. The stones that formed a circle were set up in the shape of a ring. With no truck lifts or machinery, it is almost bizarre to think about how the stones weighing 25 tonnes got in the middle of a deserted ground. According to the English folktales, the stones were transported from Ireland by the extramundane powers of Merlin the Wizard, but this is only one of the many such fabricated stories. Archaeologists say that the stones could have also been transported by the melting of glaciers. Well, that may be the most reasonable explanation. Although there is no concrete evidence about who built it, some say that the early emerging groups like Druids could have been the creators of this beauty. We turned to the stones. Could they be gossiping in silence? Hoping that we weren't the subject of discussion, we travelled back.

The café's shelves displaying food of appetising colours were enough to make anyone drool. After fuelling up, we moved to the ground that stood displaying an array of artefacts and huts with hay-strewn rooftops. The life depicted by these makeshift structures was that of the hunter-gatherer community. Various tools like spearheads, arrows, scrapers and, most importantly, the flint stones that were used to scare the wild animals away were displayed. There was a man who stood next to it disguised in the clothes of a hunter. I could not tell if the costume was fake. If it was, then it would have been from a fancy shop. He stood pretending to craft weapons and explaining how those tools came into use. The huts were constructed using the wattle and daub model, as practised during Chalcolithic times in India.

PORTSMOUTH

While exploring the vibrant coastal city of Portsmouth, with its rich maritime history and stunning waterfront views, one can't help but marvel at how this bustling port city stands in stark contrast to the serene banks of the River Clyde in Scotland, where ships have sailed for centuries. The phone buzzed. The usual cheery music was echoing from the glove compartment, but it wasn't answered till the car pulled up. "Ay! I heard you're close to Portsmouth," said a lively voice from the other side. It was my uncle's friend. "You coming down for dinner?" We took great comfort from the fat cushioned couches that were arranged in the living room's warm space. Chais, along with other snacks, was brought up in a dyed teakwood tray (the Indian way of serving guests). "It feels like a long time since I had a nice cup of homemade chai," said Appachan, his lips smacking at every sip that was taken from the cup. There was no time for the usual talk, at least not when the sun had begun to settle. The Portsmouth hill stood well above everything it surrounded, even the surrounding waters. The view of the port town was visible from the not-so-steep hill. The far-fetched view of the shimmering lights from the buildings that stood not more than a few miles away was the only light that showed until the janitor (of a nearby building) finally decided to switch on the street lights. If I had stayed home like I initially decided, I would have missed the lovely evening. We thanked my uncle's friend and family for being such wonderful hosts and for the homely food they provided us with. Thanks to Charles Dickens and his writing, his land is now known to all.

CHAPTER 7

LONDON

They say a lot about London, and as a result, travellers often raise their expectations. I, however, did not, not after discovering the existence of beautiful yet less-visited places that rarely make it onto tourist itineraries. It was these hidden gems that captivated me the most. The UK proved to be full of surprises during my trip. First when I explored the stunning landscapes of the Lake District and then again when I ventured to Windermere. London, of course, was in a league of its own. Its intricate structures seemed almost beyond human capability to create, leaving visitors in awe.

Portsmouth was a three-hour journey from London, ensuring we wouldn't arrive before sunset. However, this was no issue for me, as I knew we would make it just in time for the most exciting English breakfast - a prediction that proved true. The receptionist greeted us warmly upon our arrival. He was tall and slender, effortlessly navigating past the space that would have hindered Appachan's stout frame. "Here is the room you've booked," he said, opening the door to what appeared to be a spacious accommodation. Framed, grainy portraits hung on the walls above the bed, a gentle breeze hinting at their potential to fall upon our heads. Two double beds occupied opposite corners, separated by a wooden chest. The room boasted indirect lighting, casting a cosy ambience, with an equally well-lit bathroom stocked with essential amenities, albeit limited to tissue papers. A dark brown table stood beneath the television, which broadcasted a few Englishmen reporting the weather. A mini-refrigerator, which occupied most of the closet space, offered a selection of cold beverages. Above it, the kettle sat alongside a supply of milk powder and coffee sachets, promising the necessary ingredients for the next morning's English breakfast. Before I could further examine the room, I fell asleep and drifted into dreams of the hearty breakfast awaiting me. I managed to wake up well in time for breakfast. The hotel's restaurant awaited with a spread that exceeded my expectations. Among the offerings were freshly made sausages and hard-boiled eggs, though there was an unexpected addition - a dish of fried potatoes, seemingly out of place for a traditional English breakfast.

Staying in London was undeniably costly, a fact we were well aware of. Careful consideration was required when booking our accommodations. Some hotels boasted steep prices despite facing blank walls, while others, situated far from the city centre, necessitated traversing through less desirable areas. However, after diligent searching, we managed to secure a hotel that fit within our budget. Transportation proved convenient, with tube and tram stations nearby. What truly caught me off guard was the abundance of Indian restaurants surrounding our chosen hotel. Ajay couldn't help but express his incredulity, albeit under his breath. We found it amusing, considering we had grown accustomed to Indian cuisine back home and weren't particularly keen on indulging in it during our travels. After all, part of the joy of travelling lies in experiencing new foods, cultures, and people; missing out on that aspect feels like missing the essence of the journey itself.

Appachan managed to fulfil his mission of finding Indian restaurants without relying on technology. It seemed effortless, as every turn revealed yet another establishment serving Indian cuisine. Each time we stumbled upon one, he would discreetly clear his throat to draw our attention. The only respite came when we noticed a few English patrons occupying tables inside these restaurants. "This seems like a nice place," Appachan remarked, pausing in front of one restaurant. And indeed, it appeared so. However, the issue wasn't with the restaurant itself, nor its food or ambience, but rather with us. The essence of travelling abroad lies in immersing oneself in the authentic and vibrant cultures these places offer, which includes sampling the local cuisine. Much to our surprise, many of these Indian restaurants boasted wide glass windows, offering passers-by glimpses of the bustling activity inside. What struck us even more was the sight of English men and women dining within, and even the staff comprised predominantly of white individuals. The only reassurance came from the signboards proudly displaying names like Sharavanabhavan.

As time passed, this scenario became all too familiar, and we found ourselves increasingly disinterested in the English breakfast offerings. The expansive glass windows provided a clear view of the daily goings-on within. Whenever the bells attached to the entrance door chimed, the foreign waitstaff would swiftly appear, greeting us with a respectful namaste and flawlessly pronouncing the names of each dish. It was undeniably impressive.

The Ilford station lay just a short mile away. Each morning, the platform bustled with men and women, impeccably dressed in their finest suits, eagerly awaiting their tubes to whisk them away to work. As the train approached, its sudden arrival sent a slight tremor through the platform. The tube, London's iconic underground train system, stood as the favoured mode of transportation for vacationers and locals alike. While there are numerous transportation options available, it's wise to steer clear of the yellow taxis, which can cost a small fortune for a round trip.

"You have the cards, don't you?"

"Wait a moment," replied Amma, digging deep into the documents nestled in her haversack. "Not this one. Maybe this? No! Ah, here they are!" she exclaimed, holding two cards aloft. These weren't just any cards, nor were they enchanted, but with points loaded onto them (the Oyster card and the London Pass), they would serve as our tickets to navigate London. Convenient? Absolutely. We observed foreign passengers clutching onto colourful guidebooks tightly, wondering which mode of transportation to choose. Tubes and trams proved to be the most practical for us, but deciding which to take was always a bit of a conundrum!

The Tower Hill station, part of the Circle District line, buzzed with activity. The throng of people thickened as they made way for those boarding the approaching tubes. This time, it wasn't just business professionals in suits; the crowd was a mix of all ages. Teenagers and young adults bustled about, appearing equally preoccupied with their agendas.

Descending a flight of stairs and navigating through the illuminated tunnel, I emerged into the open space. From a distance, I gazed upon the Tower Bridge. Its suspended portion, painted in a striking blue hue, mirrored the colour of the sky above. The bridge stood before me in all its magnificence, incomparable to the bridges connecting Tower Hill and Southwark. Adorned with intricate detailing and boasting a cheerful blue shade, it was unmistakably unique. The London rush unfolded before my eyes, a scene never lacking in vibrancy. People filled the iconic red double-decker buses, taxis zipped by, and everything seemed to move swiftly around us.

"Come on, this way, please," urged my uncle, racing ahead towards the Tower of London, which was on the brink of closing. Unfortunately, our tardiness meant we missed out on visiting it. Meanwhile, cyclists pedalled in unison across the London Bridge as we retraced our steps to where the walking tour commenced - the Tower of London itself.

This historic edifice, both a royal palace and a formidable fortress, was commissioned by William the Conqueror. Within its walls lay priceless treasures, including the crown jewels, which dazzled visitors with their brilliance. Although we missed witnessing the nightly ritual known as the Ceremony of the Keys, where the castle gates are locked, I gleaned this information from a brochure I managed to collect along the way. I had plenty of these resting in my bag. I required them to curate a travel journal that I was planning to make after going back home. Among the jewels housed in the castle is the infamous Kohinoor diamond, renowned for its beauty and feared by some for its supposed curse. Legend has it that whoever possesses the diamond will not only possess the world but also suffer its misfortunes. Many rulers who owned the diamond met tragic ends, leading to speculation about its curse.

Opposite the fort loomed the imposing Shard, a 244-metre-tall skyscraper. It struck me that this juxtaposition allowed visitors a rare opportunity to witness both the ancient beauty of the Tower of London and the modern marvel of the Shard, offering breathtaking views from its summit.

As we waited for the ticket counter to open in a couple of hours, we found ourselves observing the diverse crowd - tall men in tuxedos, elegant women, and playful toddlers - until finally, the clock struck four.

There were numerous elevators, one in each corner of the building, a seemingly extravagant provision at first glance. However, it quickly became apparent just how necessary they were to accommodate the throngs of people within. As the elevator doors closed, leaving little space to move, let alone breathe, I noticed a screen above our heads displaying vibrant abstract patterns dancing to the rhythm of elevator music.

Minutes later, the doors opened to reveal the 70th floor, where patrons lounged around the glass-panelled walls, offering panoramic views of the sprawling city below. Stretching for miles on end, the buildings resembled tiny toys from this height. Bartenders deftly balanced wine glasses and fizzy drinks, their skills on full display.

We sought out an empty corner, only to be jostled by impatient tourists eager for their turn at the glass panes. Some panes were fogged up as people pressed closer to catch a glimpse of the distant horizon. Yet, the unobstructed view from 800 feet above rendered everything below seemingly manageable. The iconic red double-decker buses appeared no larger than a baby's palm. People also looked extremely tiny from above.

As the sky darkened, Appachan grew restless, his impatience palpable with each passing minute. It wasn't until Papa's arrival that I realised the time. He emerged straight from a meeting, still sporting his 'only dry wash' coat and his identity card hanging around his neck. Despite his weary eyes, he accompanied Appachan to the Duke of York theatre to watch Henrik Ibsen's Rosmersholm.

The voices of the crowd grew faint as we navigated through the dingy streets below. Although restaurants lined every corner, we sought out an Indian restaurant, successfully coming to a halt in front of one at the deserted end of the street. It was well past suppertime, nearing the witching hour.

Westminster Abbey stood as a timeless beacon amidst the towering skyscrapers that dominated the London skyline. Its antiquity made it easily distinguishable, a vintage gem nestled within the bustling city.

Initially, I found it somewhat jarring to encounter such a historic structure amidst the modernity of London. However, Westminster Abbey's roots date back to the 1040s, and its storied history made it an integral part of numerous significant occasions. From moments of profound joy to the depths of despair and even the coronation of future rulers, the Abbey had borne witness to it all. It had hosted coronations for prominent figures spanning from William the Conqueror to Queen Elizabeth, cementing its place in British history.

The cemetery surrounding the Abbey contained the remains of individuals who had contributed significantly to human progress. Figures like Isaac Newton, whose observations revolutionised our understanding of the universe, and writers whose words could evoke a myriad of emotions with mere ink on paper found their final resting place here.

Inside the Abbey, the rustic grandeur of the castle-like structure was just as awe-inspiring as its exterior. Magnificent cavernous arches adorned with rich gold details greeted visitors, while rows of red, bulbous-like candle holders lined the corridors where choirboys once sang in uniform cassocks.

Among the many poignant memorials within the Abbey, one particularly striking tribute was dedicated to an anonymous soldier who had lost his life in the First World War. On his gravestone were inscribed the solemn words:

"BENEATH THIS STONE RESTS THE BODY OF A BRITISH WARRIOR UNKNOWN BY NAME OR RANK BROUGHT FROM FRANCE TO LIE AMONG THE MOST ILLUSTRIOUS OF THE LAND AND BURIED HERE ON ARMISTICE DAY

NOV: 1920, IN THE PRESENCE OF HIS MAJESTY KING GEORGE V

HIS MINISTERS OF STATE

THE CHIEF OF HIS FORCES

AND A VAST CONCOURSE OF THE NATION THUS ARE COMMEMORATED THE MANY MULTITUDES WHO DURING THE GREAT WAR OF 1914-1918 GAVE THE MOST THAT MAN CAN GIVE LIFE ITSELF

FOR GOD

FOR KING AND COUNTRY

FOR LOVED ONES HOME AND EMPIRE FOR THE SACRED CAUSE

OF JUSTICE AND THE FREEDOM OF THE WORLD.

THEY BURIED HIM AMONG THE KING BECAUSE HE HAD DONE GOOD TOWARDS GOD AND TOWARDS HIS HOUSE."

Graves of unidentified soldiers, found in various countries, serve as poignant reminders of the sacrifices made during times of conflict. However, one rule remains consistent across these memorials: photography near the graves is strictly prohibited.

Exploring a church as vast and rich in history as Westminster Abbey requires a significant investment of time - indeed, it's said to have taken a thousand years to construct, and equally as long to fully appreciate its intricate details.

In contrast to the bustling streets of other cities, European drivers tend to be notably more patient, and the same holds true for London's bus drivers. The iconic double-decker buses, along with the convenient hop-on-hop-off service, offer travellers a leisurely means of exploring the city. With the ability to disembark at any desired destination, passengers are treated to informative titbits about each passing landmark.

As we exited the Abbey, a mighty double-decker bus approached the station, providing us with yet another opportunity to enjoy the breathtaking views of the city from above. We spotted some of the gardens featured in the game Monopoly, their vibrant colours adding to the charm of the streets below. While purchasing these properties may be effortless in the game, the real-life counterparts require a bit more effort!

Amidst these enchanting sights, we caught a glimpse of the esteemed Buckingham Palace, distinguished by the flying Union Jack - a sure sign that the queen was in residence. Much like our landlord's unique method of communication through her window blinds, the palace's flag served as a subtle indicator of its inhabitants' whereabouts.

All this sightseeing worked up quite an appetite, and the thought of a steaming cup of chai set our stomachs rumbling in anticipation.

As our hunger began to grow more pronounced, we made our way to a nearby restaurant. The waitress greeted us with sugary compliments delivered in the quintessential British accent, adding a touch of charm to our dining experience.

After a stroll, we found ourselves standing before the iconic Madame Tussauds Wax Museum. Originally founded by Madame Tussaud herself, the museum now occupies the end of the street, drawing visitors from far and wide.

Upon entering, the elevator doors revealed the statue of Marilyn Monroe in her signature pose, her hands delicately holding down her billowing dress. However, the effect was somewhat comical as a table fan positioned beneath her dress caused it to flutter like a curtain on a stormy day. Nearby, children sat in the famous red chairs from Britain's Got Talent, donning grumpy expressions as they mimicked an unhappy Simon Cowell, their foreheads furrowed in concentration.

As our tour continued, we encountered a small train emerging from a mysterious dark tunnel. The driver's cautionary tone reminded passengers to fasten their seatbelts, sparking curiosity among the bewildered tourists who settled into their seats. The ride took us past statues illuminated by vibrant lights, each figure representing individuals whose triumphs and tragedies had shaped London's rich history. Some statues seemed to whisper tales of sorrow to one another, while others wore enigmatic expressions in the subdued lighting.

Every moment of the ride through the Chamber of Horrors was unforgettable. Tourists marvelled at the meticulous detailing, with Alan, in particular, captivated by the lifelike portrayals. His fascination stemmed from a belief that he, too, could emulate the feats of superheroes, a notion that often led to misadventures. Asha aunty, ever resourceful, rummaged through her bag in search of distractions to avert potential disasters lest we find ourselves spending the night among the wax figures.

Alan's enthusiasm soared as he watched his beloved superheroes seemingly come to life before his eyes. He was completely absorbed in the immersive experience, including a surprising encounter with a drenching spray effect.

LONDON EYE

The London Eye stands as a testament to human ingenuity and innovation, its origins shrouded in mystery. While we may never know the precise circumstances that led to its creation, its eventual success is undeniable. Despite concerns about its safety, the allure of its breathtaking views has made it a beloved attraction for visitors and locals alike.

Located on the South Bank of the River Thames, the London Eye is often mistaken for a traditional Ferris wheel. However, there are key differences between the two. Ferris wheels are more gravity-oriented, allowing passengers to remain stable even when the wheel is lopsided. When it opened to the public in 2000, the London Eye became the world's first observation wheel, a title it held until the opening of the High Roller in Las Vegas. Formally inaugurated by Tony Blair in 1999, the London Eye has since become synonymous with the city's skyline.

As the Ferris wheel slowly turned, bathing us in the warm light of the sun, we marvelled at the endless flow of traffic below. The next day marked our final farewell to London as we loaded into our cars and bid adieu to the city. Our evening was spent on a river cruise along the Thames, a timeless waterway that has flowed past the Tower Bridge since ancient times. The cool breeze in the open air above calmed our minds as we listened to the guides regale us with tales of London's history, each bend of the river offering a new perspective of the city.

During the cruise, I learned about a common misconception regarding London Bridge. Despite its fame, it lacks the ornate embellishments of other bridges, leading many to confuse it with the nearby Tower of London. Nonetheless, its simplicity belies its significance, serving as a vital link in the city's infrastructure.

CHAPTER 8

STRATFORD-UPON-AVON

The plan to visit Shakespeare's birthplace, Stratford-upon-Avon, had excited Appachan from the very beginning of the trip. As a child, he would sneak away from the chores distributed among his siblings to read the books written by Shakespeare. He would first find a suitable place to read with the book safely resting in his arms. There were plenty of such places in the rubber estates, so he would go there. For a few minutes, his mind would still linger there. But a few pages later, he would get lost in the metrical patterns of Shakespeare's plays. Young Appachan would have laughed if he were given a glimpse into the future.

Shakespeare, who was born five centuries ago, is still remembered. It was well evident from the street shops. The street that once displayed all the miscellaneous things that Shakespeare must have desired to possess as a child now has his face embossed on almost everything. Shakespeare coffee mugs, Shakespeare tablecloths, and even Romeo and Juliet-inspired seasoning containers. But the sight of this street wasn't always so mesmerising. There was a time in Stratford-upon-Avon when all hell broke loose. A time when most of the rat-infested streets could only offer sights of human corpses and rats gnawing. The deadliest of plagues reigned for a long time. People were confined to their homes, and all those who got out were caught by the then-dreaded disease: The Black Death. The only ones (the plague doctors) who roamed around had to dress funny: faces covered in masks that looked like a bird's bill and the torso protected by baggy cloaks.

We saw a building on the left. It was beige in colour with horizontal and vertical wooden panels in black. The English bay windows had railings which formed diamond patterns. "This isn't his home," Appachan said. "Who's?" I asked absent-mindedly at once. "Shakespeare's, of course." From the admiration that built up in young Appachan came questions like where he lived. The answer to all these were in the fat English biographies at the library near Appachan's home. The library was the only answer to whatever piqued one's curiosity back in his day. "The books don't say anything about a joint building." He was right. The building that welcomed us wasn't Shakespeare's home, but it was a museum.

The museum showcases the First Folio, the first collected edition of Shakespeare's work. We walked into a room where a documentary played on the screen. I don't quite remember what it was about, but if my memory serves me right, it spoke of how great a man Shakespeare was and how the people of Stratford and the world still remember him. A lot of people took an interest in watching it. The rain poured down as we walked by the roads that connected the museum's exit to the house. The gardens on either side were well maintained. There were potted plants whose names I did not know. This did not come as a surprise because I never took an interest in gardening. However, I find looking at them extremely fun. "When daisies pied and violets blue and lady-smocks all silver-white and cuckoo-buds of yellow hue do paint the meadows with delight." Shakespeare's house was a merry-looking cottage at the end of Henley Street.

It must have provided great warmth during the dull winter months when crops were ruined and people starved. Lucky for this family of ten, their father was a glove maker and not a farmer. John Shakespeare had his workroom in the extended portion of his home. Half his lifetime was spent making gloves. Toy pheasants and a few other animals hung from the thatched roof above. This was to give the tourists a better idea of what everything in the house (like the hooks) were used for. The pheasants, might have been for the family dinners they had in the next room. The dining room had a lavish oak table that could seat five. A fruit basket filled with fake shiny fruits rested on the table's surface. Some parts of the house were refurbished during the Victorian era, but most of them are still centuries old. Shakespeare's old armchair (the old oak chair) can be seen even today in the corners of his house. The stairs lead to mannequins wearing ball gowns with lace ends. The ball gowns, not being congested enough, were worn over suffocating corsets. Back in those days, men and women alike entertained certain standards of beauty. The corsets were to achieve one of those. The hair was tied in buns, hidden under satin veils. Sheer purple curtains were suspended from a wooden frame above the beds. Next to the bed was a baby's cradle with two handmade boots resting on top. It, too, had laces on its end. Funny how people fancied laces back then.

The shoes were not his, obviously. They looked like a fresh pair. No dust covered the fresh, tiny shoes or the lace. "Must be new," I said, getting the closest look I could. His body rests in the old local church of Stratford: The Holy Trinity Church. Bare shrivelled branches creaked, making an effort to sway beside the resurrection cross. But no luck. Inside the church was Shakespeare's grave, buried along with his other family members. The writing in the graffiti read:

"Good friends, for Jesus' sake, forbear to dig the dust enclosed here; blessed be the man that spares these stones, and cursed be those who move my bones."

The quote, penned by Shakespeare himself, was to prevent people from moving his bones. Bones were dug up during those days when no more spaces were found in the burial grounds. The curse-like sentences threatened anyone who wished to flout the playwright's last wish.

It was 4th May of 2019. That time of the year when everybody I knew and didn't know existed bombarded the mobile screens with wishes. We decided to stay back home to celebrate my birthday. Someone had prepared the table. The table had a huge cake beautifully decorated along with a few birthday cards and presents.

CHAPTER 9

BLACKPOOL

Mummyamma's collection of rosaries occupied the different containers and pouches in the house. Beads in alabaster white were kept in small transparent boxes. The ones in the continuous shades of jade green with wooden crosses were kept in adorned pouches. Rosaries - there were plenty of them, but the one that stood out had moonstone beads. Appachan's niece (a nun) had presented it to her from Rome. It would shine while thumbing the blessed beads and had a velvet pouch of its own. Mummyamma wouldn't have much extraordinary information to share for most, but there was one that she could talk about for days on end. "This is the chapter of the divine mercy," she said, grasping a beaded rosary with importance in her tone. Mummyamma is a good storyteller. The protagonists in the tales narrated could take up any form as long as the sentence ended with "they lived happily ever after." It was one such tale (believed to be true by many) that brought us to Priston.

Priston is a countryside area close to the bath known for its Ladyewell Shrine. This shrine, famous among pilgrims, is known to be a chosen place. An old legend has it that Mother Mary had once appeared near the natural spring water that is said to have healing powers. The chapel was away from the forested village and had stained-glass windows above the altar. The wooden benches laid in the chapel were occupied. Everything grew loud with the silence. A few minutes of silent prayer were done, and a few wishes were made before the return. As my brother's passion for football grew with each passing year, a visit to Blackpool's renowned football club became an essential part of our journey.

A few minutes outside the club while on the way to the beach were enough to satisfy him. The car was parked close to the tower of Blackpool (the tall red freestanding building by the sea). The fairs on either side displayed sandcastles, beach necklaces made of seashells, and tie-dye swimsuits. The sun shone on the sand, but it wasn't sunny enough for me to get a scoop of ice cream from the nearby parlour. The five-foot-long trench coat (that I wore) was dragged along the road and moved violently with the wind. No children fought for turns to get the wafer cones that were suspended from the windows of the mobile van. There was no sign of them at all. Everyone seemed busy riding the merry-go-rounds nearby.

We decided to explore the nearby garden next. Water from the fountain sprung through the wild thorny bushes. People walked their dogs, all of them of different breeds and sizes. All was well until Alan stepped on one of the dog's tails. The ferocious growl was followed by the showing of the set of sharp white teeth it had. The next time you cuddle a dog or play with it, be careful not to touch its tail.

CHAPTER 10

The great hall displayed the train models. The train with the red bulged front was monikered the Duchess of Hamilton. The train in blue with bold gold details was the Mallard - a steam locomotive. Close to the train was another of the same, but different in model with shades of red, green, and black all over it. A round circular front with a black cylinder-shaped top front. "Thomas," I recalled as I got closer. The features that it once had in 'Thomas the Tank Engine' disappeared into the surface - now flat. Thomas stood still and cold.

We were late. No traffic or roads were to blame, but "it was the brick cold weather this time." I resisted meeting Appachan's stern stare. We were supposed to be on a train like that to tour York, but in the National Railway Museum, we stood dumbfounded by the train models that once ruled the rails.

LIVERPOOL AND MANCHESTER

Liverpool, in my memory, wasn't included in our long list of destinations, but it did make it to the list eventually. It was again a narration that got us there. Funny how influential stories can get! Where were we to travel next? "Liverpool," Amma said, her mind already made up. Conversations sparked up, not knowing what exactly built up the excitement for a small port town.

CHEESES FROM LIVERPOOL

One morning, three friends argued about what to eat for breakfast. Finally, they came to have a common view. They had eggs, ham, jam, butter, cold meat, bread, and small pieces of cheese. The cheese had a very specific smell. And Jay remembered a story when one of his friends bought cheese at Liverpool.

Amma had recalled the story without much effort. The author had mentioned it (cheese) as an object of exuded odour. Harris (one of the protagonists) transports the mouldy cheese that is so full of stench to his friend Tom. The people in the train compartment find it difficult to bear the stench and instantly shift to the other vacant seats. Could anything big or small be subjected to such bad repute? We had to find out for ourselves.

Liverpool, a port city in the Northwestern part of England was what excited us next. This city was a blend of dissimilar cultures and buildings. The concrete buildings were of both rustic and modern architecture, bringing it both a London and a Glaswegian touch. Some boys of my brother's age walked down the lane. The bright red jerseys exposed their russet-toned arms. What else would I see people wearing apart from jerseys in a football dominant city?

Manchester - another city known among football fans was where we spent the last few days. The suffix Chester (translates into the Roman word for fortification) is added to most well-known places in England. This well-known fact was not known to me until upon my return to India. As a fan of Manchester United, Ajay's only intention of the visit was to cheer live for the football players he had been wanting to meet. The tickets arrived on the 10th of May, and the much-awaited match day soon arrived. He was given a few pounds, and an additional five pounds to meet any worst-case scenario. We saw him off after he promised to return before curfew. He kept his word, but when he came back in the evening, his face was visibly disappointed. The team he supported had suffered a crushing defeat, one unlike any they had faced before. "Was this trip really worth it?" he asked, his expression reflecting utter dejection. However, his day was not entirely unpleasant. There was a commotion at the exit involving a crowd and some burly men. "They were shielding someone from the mob. It was John Bradley West. His slicked-back hair was meticulously groomed, and he flashed a smile in my direction," Ajay recalled. I remained skeptical until he showed me a photograph of the two of them together.

CHAPTER 11

WALES

"Llanfairpwllgwyngyll," said Papa, his mouth making a sincere effort to spit up the eighteen-syllable word. The sheep bleated in the background. The car moved forward, ignoring the signboards in Welsh - a language we weren't conversant with. The road trip this time was to Wales. The land that narrates mythical lores of great potential, but somehow, some of them still haven't made it out of Wales. They would make great bedtime stories. One such story that lingers around in Wales is that of Mary. Not your neighbour Mary or anyone you are well informed about, but a determined girl who, at the age of fifteen, travelled 26 miles barefoot to buy a Welsh Bible. A Bible or any book, for that matter, was considered a luxury back then. This determined girl didn't give up until she bought it. This country towards the South West of the United Kingdom is known not only for its inspiring tales with determined protagonists but also for the UK's longest-named town -

Llanfairpwllgwyngyll, and a copious amount of castles, out of which a majority are in shambles.

The time ticked by slowly, and the tramway was seen approaching the Great Orme tramway station. It looked like two undersized compartments in blue. Its windows with no glass panes let the cold breeze in. The numbness could have been avoided had we gotten our cardigans with us, but only rubbing our hands would work then. The tramway steered high to the summit. The alluring view on either side also increased as it did. Houses in a subtle beige colour formed the borders of the sea-brink. On the other side, one could see the roughness of the cliffs, its threatening ends protruding out into the tramway track. The summit provided an even better view of the land below. The serene waters and the green hills were looked at once again. Walking down, shops were spotted. Postcards, paper maps, and souvenirs were displayed on the shop front. The furnishing was minimal but inviting. The cosy atmosphere created by the two amiable couples called me in. The owner was a man of few words, or so I thought, but it qualified as an assumption. He barely interrupted, but when he was given a chance, he spoke of everything that the documentation (that was up for sale) could fit in.

The confab soon switched to Elephants. He remembered reading about them in a book and called them 'mighty mammals'. The couple went on to talk about a lot of things especially about the diverse culture that India was so full of. "Have a good day!" they said when every fact was poured out. "Wish you the same!" I said before returning to the tram. The weather continued to grow wild. Mothers hugged their children tight, and Alan leaned back on Appachan's shoulders. He suddenly leapt from the latter's lap when a hostile horned goat was seen from out the window. "Ash! That, my Alan dear, is a billy goat. Heard of one?" Alan's disappointing nods said he hadn't. The goat was foraging for grass when the curious eyes of the onlookers interrupted him. "Who knows," continued Appachan, "he might have been the clever billy goat who escaped from entering the troll's tummy." Goodbye, Billy. Have a nice time hunting at the dry cliff rock summit.

The US has thrift stores, but in Britain, goods are displayed in the trunks of mobile vans. Vehicles were parked adjacent; the trunk doors were kept open to display miscellaneous items with revised price tags attached to them. Tiny decors and wooden catapults for when the mango tree bears fruits were kept with every other object. Mothers had their eyes set on floral quilts. Fathers looked for vacant seats, and children stood beside them, pleading for objects that brought only a fleeting moment of pleasure. The prices quoted were reasonable, unlike the Trafford Centre. It was kept for the last like every best thing, but it wasn't the most predominant of reasons. A shopping spree would be on the last list of priorities in an expensive city like Manchester. It was the biggest of all shopping complexes in the UK, with over two hundred shops under one roof. The expensive-looking dresses adorned the mannequins and added to the expensive-looking interior. "With an interior like that of a castle, you can never whine about not being able to run a shopping spree," said Appachan, distracting us from objects on either side. There were dolphin-shaped fountains, and water sprayed up from their mouths. There wasn't anything particularly remarkable about it, but there was one thing that left me puzzled and unable to find an explanation – a piano that seemed possessed. It played by the side, the keys pressing without the need for a pianist. A crowd stood by, equally confused as us to find the piano playing on its own.

The ceiling of the complex was adorned with streaks of light palette shades. Clouds were painted onto the ceiling. Behind the dreamy clouds flew angels striking the strings of harps.

"Your order is ready," came a stranger's voice that made us look back. He carried a brown paper bag that contained the ramen noodles that had us waiting. The seasoning that overpowers this dish is from the clear broth (sometimes brown), depending on the soup base. We found a sheer number of other vibrant ingredients that might seem uncanny in a one-dish meal. The authentic Asian meal is served in a bowl to prevent the broth from spilling. The authentic way of eating ramen noodles is with chopsticks, but people are allowed to choose the cutlery that suit their preferences. So, if you are an amateur chopstick user, then feel free to use whatever you are familiar with (because why poke an eye out of an innocent person?).

The days of my vacation came to an end. The suitcases were dusted out again, and some who volunteered to pack disappeared on the day of packing (note: I was not throwing shade at my dear brother). My cousin brother, Alan, was tucked into his bed when we went to kiss him goodbye. My uncle dropped us at the same airport from where we began the trip. My eyes teared up. I was happy that the trip turned out better than I had anticipated, but there was a part of me that knew I would miss that place. I turned around to croon a final goodbye to my uncle and the city of Manchester.

It was getting towards 11 PM when we arrived. As expected, what awaited us was heavy traffic. No car could move. As I sat in the car, I thought of school, and it got me in high spirits (which was quite unusual coming from me). In the next hour, our car moved about a metre, but this was huge progress considering how closely packed all the cars were. Would Monday blues return? I didn't have an answer to that, but it would take another few hours until I saw my inviting bed next. I watched the headlights blink and observed the place until Appachan broke the silence by saying, "Back in the UK, you won't see so much of traffic or road rage." He was not wrong.

I prepared to sleep. I closed my eyes and thanked God for the great trip that was made possible.